Poem Noir:
A Celebration of Film Noir in Poetry

Other Books by This Author from Third Coast Press

Small Poems
Michigan Gothic

(Available at Barnes and Noble, Amazon and Lulu)

Poem Noir
A Celebration of Film Noir in Poetry

David Jibson

Third Coast Press
2014

Copyright © 2014 by David Jibson

All rights reserved. This book or any portion thereof may not be reproduced or used in any manner whatsoever without the express written permission of the publisher except for the use of brief quotations in a book review or scholarly journal.

First Printing: 2014

ISBN 978-312-57195-2

Third Coast Press
1320 Astor Ave. #1712
Ann Arbor, Michigan 48104

Comments and discussion are welcome at this e-mail address:

jibsond@yahoo.com

Dedication

To my readers and the poets of The Crazy Wisdom Poetry Circle and the West Side Writer's Gang who have been so encouraging and helpful along the way.

Contents

Introduction ix
Dark City 3
Mr. Big 4
Torch Singer 5
Gorillas 6
Don't Forget Your Hat 7
Her 8
Floater 9
Poem Noir 10
Get in the Car 17
Pitfall 18
D.O.A. 19
Getaway 20
Whit Bissell 22
The Dark 23
The Third Man 24
Hyde 25
Mr. K 26
Wrong Turn on Scarlet Street 28
Plastic Surgery Noir 29
Death by Poison 31
Lady on a Train 32
A Villanelle 33
The Mad Scientists Daughter 34

Thin Man	35
House Dick	36
To Have and Have Not	37
About the Author	38

Introduction

"It was a dark and stormy night," as cartoonist Charles Schultz's *Snoopy* began each of his fictional crime novels. Poem Noir is a labor of love that reflects my affinity for this uniquely American genre of film, perhaps the only truly organic Hollywood artistic movement.

Inside this book you will find many of the characters, plot devices, twists and turns of noir films, both real and imagined, – all expressed as poetry. Hard boiled detectives, seductive sirens, mugs, thugs, gangsters and crooked cops populate the pages of a dark and mysterious city.

Buy yourself popcorn, sit back in your chair and claim the arm rests on both sides of your seat. The newsreel, the cartoons and the previews of coming attractions have been shown. It's time for our main feature.

-David Jibson

Dark City

Dark City is a mighty beast,
a sprawling monster
with a skeleton of steel
covered in a concrete overcoat.

In Dark City laws and souls
are trampled in the street.
The strong eat the weak.
Lives dangle from dangerous heights.

Living here is a fevered dream.
A man can go off his nut on these streets
among the jaundiced cops,
corrupt politicians, psychotic crooks.

In the city's tenderloin the seedy rooms
are clammy with the residue
of spoiled hopes, abandoned dreams,
wallpaper that sweats fear.

Everywhere is the crackle and buzz
of neon signs that stare each other down
across dirty streets
and grimy infected avenues.

Dark City is a mighty beast
with a taste for human flesh,
your flesh if you make a wrong turn.
That bullet in your forehead
was meant to slow you down.

Mr. Big

Harry the Horse says,
"The Boss wants to see you."
Ordinarily I'd decline his invitation
but he's got his hand in his coat pocket
and something in it is pointed at my chest.

Everybody wants to see Mr. Big
when they want to see him.
Nobody wants to see Mr. Big
when he wants to see them.

He's the pope of the city.
Everybody kisses the big diamond he wears
on the manicured pinky of his right hand.

From his office in the back of the nightclub
Mr. Big runs the dark side of the city.
He owns the mayor, the chief of police,
most of the city council,
even fifty percent of the governor.

He understands that anyone
who is his friend is also his enemy,
that loyalty walks a tight-wire
stretched between greed and fear.

He's Genghis Khan, Alexander,
Napoleon, Caesar, and Ivan The Terrible
ground up and rolled into one fat little sausage.
Just one of those gigantic cigars that he smokes
is worth more than your life.

Torch Singer

Hers is the saddest story.
You can hear it in the songs she sings,
her honey-alto voice thicker than the smoke
that obscures her pretty face on the stage.

No man in the room can resist
falling for her, falling for her hard.
She's a living siren in a low cut gown,
sparkling bracelets, exotic hair.

On the final note her lower lip trembles,
her dark eyes grow sadder, more plaintive.
She leaves you with the false impression
she wants you to take her home with you.

That's why Mr. Big hired her,
to keep you coming back for more,
to keep you drinking, keep you drowning,
making sure you can't stay away.

Gorillas

We don't know what their mother's called them.
We know them by handles like Whitey,
Slim, Shorty, Bugs, Mugsy and Rocky.

Two of them are permanently on guard
outside Mr. Big's office door
in the back of the night club.

One of them chews on a toothpick.
The other tosses a silver dollar
over and over, always coming up heads.

They're mugs, henchmen, hoodlums,
goons, gorillas, muscle,
hoods in black fedoras.

They want to take you for a ride
but not before they've broken
a few of your ribs.

They're a couple of empty suits,
afraid of nothing except for their
hat-check-girl and dime-a-dance girlfriends.

Don't Forget Your Hat

When you need to know who's who and what's what
in this town, get to know the hat check girl at Mr. Big's.
She rubs elbows with the best and the worst:
the millionaire bankers and street thugs,
the gamblers, gangsters and high society wags,
the artsy set, the Hollywood stars,
the phony tipsters and juggernauts of Wall Street.
She knows them all and she knows their business.

She's a friendly small town girl
from one of those states that begins with an *I*.
She came to the city to be a dancer.
but all she found were a lot of bright lights
and empty promises. She took the only work she could get.
It barely pays the bills but she'll be okay
because surviving here is all about what you know
and, believe me, she knows plenty.

Don't fall for that simple country girl act.
That's just her way of seeming harmless.
And don't ever give her the double-cross.
The dame's got friends - if you know what I mean.

Her

*I didn't want any part of her
but I kept smelling that jasmine in her hair.*
- Humphrey Bogart in *Dead Reckoning* (1947)

Money's not the root of all evil.
She is. I would kill for her,
me, an easy going guy all my life
but not anymore. Not since I met her.

I said I would kill for her and I know I would
because I already have;
I have and I will again if I have to
and it looks as though I will.

I hate her more than I hate myself
and, believe me, that's plenty.
I guess this'll be the end of us both
and it'll be her fault:
Her and that damned smell of jasmine.

Floater

He was dressed in a cheap suit,
an old one, frayed at the collar and cuffs,
loose fitting, lapels too wide.
He'd been in the water a couple of days
according to the medical examiner on the scene.
The bullet hole in his chest suggested
a cause of death other than drowning.

That he was found at all
was a matter of pure chance.
The river usually carries these floaters out to sea,
food for the carrion eaters of the deep.

There was no wallet in his pocket,
no laundry marks on his shirt,
nothing that said, *this is who I was*
except for a book of matches
from a dingy gin joint downtown.
The cops will start there
and give up after nobody I. D.s him.

There were some bruises on his ribs.
Marks on his wrists say they had been tied.
The scar on his cheek was an old one.
He doesn't match any missing persons report.
Chances are there won't ever be one;
not by a mother he barely knew,
or the sometimes girlfriend
who wouldn't see him for weeks on end
and certainly not by his former boss, Mr. Big,
who never bothered to ask him his real name.

Poem Noir

Scene 1: *The Big Sleep*

This is a night for fog stalking the back streets and alleys
as dangerous as the Jack The Ripper himself.
A night you become a hard-jawed detective from a 30s novel
prowling the streets of old China Town
following up leads in the case of a missing heiress.

It's a night for sitting in a diner at two A.M.
where the blond waitress knows you as Mike
and you think maybe she wouldn't mind knowing
you are thinking about those Betty Grable legs
to the tops of her stockings and beyond.

The door of the diner opens, a thug walks in.
"Fat Man" is all the name you know him by.
He's given you trouble in the past
and you wonder if he followed you here on purpose.

Maybe this is the night he tries to measure you
for a pair of cement overshoes,
the night of *the big sleep*.

You feel for the comforting bulge
of the thirty-eight under your coat.
The Fat Man looks the joint over
through tiny pig eyes and leaves without a word.

This is a night you wish Lulu was back in town,
a night the color's been bled from the world
and you live your life as film noir.
Your mind goes back to the blond and those legs
but you've dodged enough danger for one night.

This is the night you finally realize
despair is the best thing that's ever happened to you
and the scream of the night hawk
is all the company you've ever needed.

Scene 2: *The Maltese Falcon*

Blondie asks if you want another cup of java.
You give her the once over a little too long.
She winks or was it something in her eye?
She turns her back to you and bends over,
pretends she's picking something off the floor.
Yeah, it's a message, a nice round message
with a glimpse of garter as an exclamation point.

But there's the matter of a missing heiress
somewhere out there lost in the wretched fog
and Mr. Big is willing to pay
a year's office rent for you to find her.
You grab your damp fedora and shove off.
"Keep your motor running honey. I'll be back."
You're not sure if you said it or thought it.
It doesn't matter. You know she'll be here.

In the warehouse district there's an old man.
They say he was a player on the docks
but he went blind during prohibition
soaking up too much Jamaica Ginger.
It left him blind and doing the Jake Walk
but his ears are good. He hears everything.
It's time you paid him a little visit.

As you near the corner the old man haunts
you hear footsteps down a dark brick alley,
the footsteps of a man in a hurry.
Some punk in gray nearly knocks you over.
He pulls a cap down over his blank eyes,
runs down the street and around the corner.

You turn up the alley to see just why
the punk is so anxious to get away.
A pair of feet point up at the dim light
tossed casually into the thick fog
by a single naked electric bulb.
As you get closer you can see the old man
and you can tell from the blade in his chest
he's as old as he's ever going to get.
A pool of blood spreads from underneath him,
black as a *Maltese Falcon* in the dark.

There's nothing anyone can do for him now.
Too bad he got it before he could talk
and tell you what you needed to know.
But maybe he can tell you one last tale.
That knife handle with the ivory dragon,
you've seen one just like it somewhere before.

Scene 3: *The Lady from Shanghai*

The top guy in China Town is Woo Fong.
He runs a jazz club called The Old Shanghai.
It's not your kind of joint as a rule
but its popular with a certain crowd
of idle rich and a few artsy types.

The place is exotic, dark and smoky.
You walk in and take a seat at the bar.
A Chinese bartender asks what you'll have.
"I need to see Woo Fong," you tell the boy.
"Wait right here," he says. "I'll see if he's in."

He comes back soon and says to follow him.
He leads you to a room far in the back,
opens a curtain and gestures you in.
Woo sits on a divan against one wall,
on either side a beautiful young girl,
his bodyguards according to rumor.
Either one could easily crush your spine
with a single blow from a tiny fist.

The Chinaman looks like a small Buddha
with a thin mustache and pointed goatee.
He motions you to sit and before you speak
he knows who you are and why you're here.
"You need to see the Lady from Shanghai.
She'll be singing out front in a moment."

You're led out to the main room of the club,
sat at a table in front of a stage.
In a moment or two a drink appears,
the lights go dim, a combo starts to play.
On the stage the most beautiful woman
you've ever seen starts to sing a torch song.
When it ends the audience is too drunk
on the sound of her voice to applaud.

She steps down and walks to your table,
perches rather than sits on a chair,
a fragile and enigmatic sparrow.
"I understand you've been looking for me
but you should know I don't want to be found.
Tell the man that you call Mr. Big
that I'm dead or gone which ever you want."

The story she tells you gives you the shakes,
how her missionary parents were killed
by the "I Ho Ch'uan" or what we call
the Fists of Righteousness or The Boxers.
How she was saved by a cousin of Woo
who hid her out in an old potter's shed.

After weeks of hiding they smuggled her
down to the docks on an ox drawn cart
in a giant yellow porcelain jar
and loaded the jar onto a freighter
bound for California where Woo waited.

But a black-hearted ship's captain
diverted the tub to a different port.
"So I'm no heiress," she says to you,
"I was sold to the one you call Mr. Big
and kept like a pet in a gilded cage".

"It took years for Woo and his family
to trace me to Big and his mansion.
The two ninja bodyguards that you saw
carried out the final rescue mission."

But what is her real name you want to know.
"I have no name as far as anyone knows.
Just call me The Lady from Shanghai."
With that she disappears into the smoke
and nothing's left for you to do but leave.

Scene 4: *Angels With Dirty Faces*

When you leave the club it's early dawn.
The deadly night fog is starting to lift.
You're faced with the job of telling Mr. Big
you're quitting the job, that his beauty's trail
went cold and finally came to an end.
Now for that diner and some steak and eggs.
Blondie should be about done with her shift.

The streets are empty still at this hour.
A delivery van rumbles up the street.
As you near the diner a figure appears,
a woman in a rain coat with scarf covered head.
She reaches into a bag slung over one arm.
The glint of a chrome barrel stings your eyes.

She points the gun directly at your head.
You instinctively start to raise your hands.
She says, "keep 'em down and hold very still."
There's the flash of a muzzle and loud report.
They say that dead men never hear the shot;
the speed of the bullet is faster than sound.
Behind you the sound of the thud of a body,
the Fat Man drops hard to the cement.
The knife he intended for you clanks to the ground.

Then you can see it's the blond with the gun.
She walks up to you and pulls out of the bag
a brick sized package wrapped in brown paper.
From the size and weight you know that it's cash.
She says, "This is for you, courtesy of
The Lady From Shanghai as she calls herself."

"She says not to bother contacting Mr. Big.
He met with an accident late last night."
The blond then smiles and says there's one thing more,
"plugging The Fat Man, that one's on me.
Woo hired me to keep an eye glued on you.
But he never said a word to me
about saving your life or your skin."

Your last words to her, "thank god for angels,
blond *angels with dirty faces.*"
You close your eyes as she walks away
memorizing the sound of her heels clicking
and fading slowly among the sounds
of the city you love coming to life.

The End - Music up - Fade to Black - Roll Credits

Get in the Car

The Professor had all the angles figured,
at least that's what he thought.
It would be an easy caper he said.
Bust through the basement wall,
blow the jewelry store safe,
a million bucks, in an out in ten minutes.

But he hadn't figured on the alarms next door
going off when we blew the safe.
Sure, he knew about French poetic realism,
Jacobean tragedy and
structuro-semiological judgment,
stuff that could make your head explode,
but he didn't know beans
about alarms or cops with guns.

Once a deal gets queered,
that's when things get interesting.
Well I'm not running anymore.
I'm through with being a cheap chiseler.
What about you, Doll?
You in or out?

We're improvising from here.
If you don't have the stomach for it
get in the car and drive. Drive fast.
Get yourself out of this *Asphalt Jungle*
while you still can.

Pitfall

I feel like a wheel
within a wheel within a wheel.
I want to leave the house this morning
and drive to South America.
I read where they have a road all the way
to South America now.

I've been on the straight and narrow
my whole life. You were the prettiest girl in school.
I was voted most likely to succeed.
Something more should happen
to people like us.

One day I won't walk through that door
of the Olympic Insurance Company at nine sharp.
Everything will be different.
Everything will be better.
I don't want to be one of fifty million.
I'm sick of being part of the backbone of America.

D. O. A.

Who's in charge here? I want to report a murder.
It took place yesterday in San Francisco.

No, I'm not a witness. I'm the victim.
Well, you're right I'm not dead yet, but soon.

I don't know but pretty soon, any time now. If not today
tomorrow for sure but probably by tonight.

Okay then, I want to report an attempted murder.
In a little while you can call it a murder.

Several people were involved.
Sure, one was a dame. There's always a dame.

The guy who did it? Halliday was his name.
No, he's dead. I shot him.

Of course it was justified. He killed me first.
All I did was notarize a bill of sale.

No, I wasn't worried about that.
I figured I'd be dead before you could arrest me.

Yes, I would like to sit down. I don't feel so good...

Getaway

Stealing the Model A was the easy part.
Souping it up took a couple of days.
Henry Ford had done most of the work.
The finishing touches were up to *Driver*.

He made his name running white lightnin'
from Hazard to Chicago.
No cop car ever came close to him.
He was the best wheel man in the country.

By nine A.M. Driver has the car parked
in front of Merchant's bank,
motor purring like a cheetah,
Driver wearing his lucky gloves.

At 9:05 he starts to worry. Then it happens.
A big limo pulls up beside him, double parks him in.
Before he can do anything about it
the bank's alarms start to ring.

Four masked gunmen run out shooting.
Eddie The Earl is limping.
Crackers Lafferty's shirt is covered in blood.
He drops to his knees halfway to the car.

Chicken Charlie gets it next in the back.
Then Rat Face Freddy Malone goes down.
Driver guns the engine, pops the clutch.
The only place he can go is onto the sidewalk.

The Ford leaps up and over the curb.
The left front fender takes out a mailbox.
In the middle of the block he knocks off a hydrant
before he swerves back into the street.

The rear window explodes from a swarm of bullets.
Driver's head hits the wheel hard,
his face pressed down on the horn.
His foot mashes hard on the gas.

The ford leaps the curb on the other side,
glances off a lamp post,
slams head-on through the front windows
of Leo's Fine Haberdashery Shop.

By the time the cops get there
Driver is breathing his last breath,
forms the word *mama* with his lips
but no sound comes out.

Whit Bissell

It was home of the Tarzan double feature
with Johnny Weissmuller or Gordon Scott
Jock Mahoney or Lex Barker,
Cartoon Capers, bad film noir
and on Fridays as many as you could pile
into an Oldsmobile got in for a buck.

It was a place treasure was kept
late summer evenings
before anyone thought to save daylight
rather than spend it.

Monsters from black lagoons in rubber suits
aliens with helmets that looked like
basketballs painted silver
Attacks by blobs of gelatinous goo,
fifty foot women,
irradiated grasshoppers,
atomic ants.

And lording over it all,
greatest of the B movie actors.
Whit Bissell the doctor.
Whit Bissell the top general of the air force.
Whit Bissell the scientist,
who finally figures out how to save humanity.

Whit Bissell, the voice of authority,
the voice of calm in the face of death.
Whit Bissell the voice of certainty.
Yes, we can survive. Yes, we must survive
for the sake of human kind.

The Dark

As many things exist in the dark
as do in the light
and, who knows, maybe more.
It is the possible discrepancy
that worries us.

The Third Man

There was a third man on the street that night.
Witnesses say there were only two
but I was there and saw
Harry die for the first time.

The brick street wore the sheen of rain.
The car was black. It was speeding.
The driver never touched the brakes.
There was no screeching sound,
no tire marks left behind.

Harry never saw it coming.
None of us did until it was too late.
So don't believe what you hear.
There was a third man on the street that night.
I was the third man, but who am I?
Let's just say the answer to that question
was buried in a cold cemetery in Vienna
somewhere near the body of Harry Lime.

Hyde

> *Perhaps you prefer a gentleman. One of those panting hypocrites who like your legs but talk about your garters.*
>   -Fredric March as Mr. Hyde (1931)

To be perfectly honest,
I haven't been feeling myself lately.
Doctor Jekyll hasn't made a diagnosis
but he's trying different medications
hoping some combination of them will help.

I can describe the worst of the symptoms.
People say I've been irritable.
I wake up mornings soaked in sweat.
I find hair growing in the oddest places.

My girlfriend says she doesn't know me.
People who should recognize me
act like they've never seen me before.
I've been tired during the day like I haven't slept.

Tonight I'm locking myself in.
I've heard rumor that some of my friends
are planning an intervention
but I swear everything I take is by prescription.

Mr. K.

They appeared out of nowhere
at six in the morning.
The tall one stood silent nearest the door.

The shorter one took a place
at the center of the room.
"Mr. K.," he said.

"Who are you,
how did you get in here?"

"Who do you think we are Mr. K.?"
His face was bland as a monk fish
a few days out of water.

"I'm sure I don't know.
What is it you want?"

"We're here to inform you
you're under arrest, Mr. K.
Will you please get dressed?"

"Arrest on what charge?
What have I done?
Who is accusing me of a crime?"

"What do you think
you have done, Mr. K?"

"Why, I have done nothing.
I have broken no law.
I have done nothing, nothing at all.
And what is it you are writing in that note book?"

"It's your confession, Mr. K.
I'm taking everything down as evidence for the trial."

"Trial for what, confession to what?
I told you, I have done nothing,
nothing at all."

"Exactly, Mr. K, that's
what I put down. Now
will you please get dressed?"

Wrong Turn on Scarlet Street

It's easy in a strange neighborhood
in the night city to make that one wrong turn
onto a narrow street
you've never been down before.

Life is like that sometimes.
One minute you're at a party
honoring your twenty-five years of service
to mediocrity and boredom.

The next minute you're lost
and looking for a way back home.
But there is no way back home
once you've made that wrong turn.

You realize somewhere along the way
you've grown old and ugly,
that your life is a prison,
your own conscience, the warden.

Then comes that one night
you see a chance to bust out
so you take it and from there
fate drags you down that evil street.

Once you've sold your life and your soul
you can never buy them back
even if you can steal enough to afford them.
All sales are final on Scarlet Street.

Plastic Surgery Noir

I knock the pattern on the wooden door
just as I was instructed, three long, two short.
The doctor opens it a thin crack,
the smell of gin on his breath.
I say the secret word that I can't repeat here.
The door opens wide. He pokes his head out,
cranes his neck to look both ways
up and down the dim hallway
making sure I wasn't followed,
stands aside and motions me in.

The windows are closed, the shades drawn.
"Names are not important," he says,
"except for who sent you".
"Rocky sent me," I tell him. He nods,
asks if I have the money on me.
I hand him two hundred in twenties.
He holds one of them up to a bare light bulb
that hangs from the ceiling
to check that it's legit. It is.

I tell him I need a new face.
He starts pinching my five-o'clock shadowed cheeks,
twists my nose between his yellow fingers.
"I can do that," he says.
"Maybe improve on this mug of yours."

He tells me I'll be in bandages for six weeks,
can only eat soup through a straw.
He leads me into a back room,
his operating theater. Scalpels are laid out
on metal trays. He pours ether on a towel.
"Let's get started," he says.

I wake up, my face burning with pain.
I'm on a bare mattress in some other room.
There's a mirror. My head is wrapped like a mummy,
narrow slits for my eyes and mouth.

Six weeks pass like a century. I've lost thirty pounds.
I play solitaire, read the papers, play more solitaire,
lose a sawbuck to the doc playing gin rummy.
Finally the day comes for the bandages to come off.

The process of unwinding takes a long time.
The doc stands back in a drunken weave,
stares at me awhile, pronounces his success,
hands me a cracked tortoise shell mirror.
I hold it up in front of me, staring at my new face.
Lauren Bacall stares back.

Death by Poison

I love the way this poem starts out
at the farthest end of a long curving gravel drive
lined with ancient elms that leads to a manor house.
And I especially love that no rain is expected
before the fourth stanza.

The Edwardians were so refined,
unlike like the Victorians for whom the sun
never seemed to shine
and who took everything so seriously.

And unlike the Elizabethans
in their oh so uncomfortable clothes,
and those smirky looks about what really
lay underneath all those codpieces.

I prefer the Edwardians in their formal gardens,
playing croquet on manicured lawns,
gin and tonics in their hands.
Now comes that rain, right on schedule,
meaning old Lord Carrington is about to die
a horrible death by poison.

Lady on a Train

There is a lady on a train,
a train through the city.
She watches out the window,
sees taxis on the street,
vendors on the sidewalk,
couples walking arm in arm,
children playing stick ball,
a dog eating from a trash can,
a murder in an office building.

What can she do?
She's on a train.
She calls the police from the station.
They go to the building,
find no dead body.
The lady on the train must be crazy.

But I believe her
because she's pretty.
I will sit here in a darkened room
for as long as it takes
to figure out the mystery.
Maybe we're both crazy.

A Villanelle

the flying saucers have landed
in every capitol of the world
alien forces are everywhere and we are screwed

the Eiffel Tower has vaporized
the Kremlin is a pile of stone
the flying saucers have landed

Washington's monument lays on its side
Lincoln's Memorial is blown to dust
our defenses are destroyed and we are screwed

every one of our soldiers is gone
the green rays have turned them all to ash
the flying saucers have landed

Big Ben in London is rubble now
the Golden Gate is a twisted wreck
Lake Michigan is boiled away and we are screwed

Tokyo and Beijing have been set ablaze
hopeless refugees fill the pews of every church
the flying saucers have landed
and we are screwed

The Mad Scientists Daughter

I once fell for the daughter of a mad scientist.
It seems all mad scientists have a daughter;
a beautiful daughter with pointed breasts,
a tight sweater and no mother.

If the daughters are beautiful
chances are their mothers were beautiful too,
but we will never know for sure
because nobody has ever seen one.

Thin Man

Nick is drunk before the train even leaves the station.
He says it prevents motion sickness.
After martini number four he is passed out
in the seat of the private compartment.

Asta sits with his chin on his paws
watching Nora fuss with the feathers
of her newest hat. Nick begins to snore.
Nora tickles his face with a feather.

He rouses enough to lean the other way,
calls for another round in his sleep.
Nora gathers Asta up in her arms,
heads for the bar car with a sigh and a frown.

When she returns an hour later
Nick is sitting with a well stacked blonde who says
she wants to hire Nick to find her missing fiance.
Nora isn't jealous. Nick is impotent.

House Dick

He was a flatfoot until a Sargent caught on
that he was shaking down the shop owners
on his beat. It seems the department frowns on that,
at least when you aren't willing to share the profits.

He tried the private eye thing for a while,
had a second story office over a Chinese laundry,
failed at that because he couldn't keep his hands off
the wives that husbands were paying him to follow.

Now he sits all day under a potted palm
in a flophouse lobby
hidden behind a racing form
ready to crack wise or take a bribe
from any mug with a sawbuck
who wants to bring in a girl with no wedding ring.

There's not much glamor in the job
but, what the hell, somebody's gotta do it.
And besides, it beats wearing out the leather
on the soles under his big flat feet.

If you're someone who matters
he can be a good guy to know.
For a few bucks he can find a way
to keep your name out of the papers.

To Have and Have Not

In the balcony rows where the lovers sit
it's not so far from heaven
where the beam from a projector
slices the darkness and we,
playing at Bogie and Bacall,
splash ourselves up on the screen,
an etching of a former world,
where we wish we could
live out our lives in two dimensions
in the deep shadows of a darkened theater,
the objects of every envy.

About the Author

David Jibson lives in Ann Arbor, Michigan. He is a member of The Crazy Wisdom Poetry Circle and The Poetry Society of Michigan. His poetry has been published in the literary journals *Third Wednesday, The Brasilia Review* and *Peninsula Poets*.